The Wire

Also by Michael Zand

lion : the iran poems

The Shearsman Chapbook Series, 2012

Seren Adams : *Small History*
Kit Fryatt : *Rain Down Can*
Mark Goodwin : *Layers of Un*
Alan Wall : *Raven*
Michael Zand : *The Wire & other poems*

hors de série
Shira Dentz : *Leaf Weather*

The Wire
& other poems

Michael Zand

Shearsman Books

First published in the United Kingdom in 2012 by
Shearsman Books
50 Westons Hill Drive
Emersons Green
BRISTOL BS16 7DF

Shearsman Books Ltd Registered Office
30–31 St. James Place, Mangotsfield, Bristol BS16 9JB
(this address not for correspondence)

www.shearsman.com

ISBN 978-1-84861-249-5
First Edition

Acknowledgements
Special thanks to Tim Atkins, Sean Bonney, Steven Fowler, Tony Frazer,
Harry Gilonis, Sebastian Groes, Jeff Hilson, Peter Jaeger, Antony John,
Ariel Kahn, Sarah Kelly, Mimi Khalvati, Hanif Kureishi, SL Mendoza,
Stephen Mooney, Aaron Neil, Tommy Peeps, Nat Raha, Marcus Slease,
Linus Slug, Samir El-Youssef and especially Carolyn Zand
for their interest and support.

Contents

For Thomas Kian

The Wire

January

Little Gidding. The village is in mourning.
They form an orderly line.
For once, there is snow. And it bunkers.
Shovels. A few words.
Clenched.
An intensity of birds round the highest house.
Paper, scissors, stone.
Reflections of clouds against the ice make the air seem blue.
Blurred.

The Nene is part frozen, part broken.
Like a barrier. It barriers. There's also a lock here.
Boats that were first moored in the dark.
Memories. Of her, Brother.
Distanced.

Inside.
The bathroom mirror. Cracking now, like tundra.
I'm the Old Testament.
I'm Jerome looking startled in candlelight.
And aye, we were there, in our thousand-year coats.

As you say Brother, it's the Middle Ages.

A dead honeybee sits on the sill.
"Always give them what they want", you tweet.
In my mind's I.
It helps me realise, y'know. You.
It helps me realise that when you are, when you are.
It helps me realise that when you speak.
It hurts.
Like the limes of Jericho.

Later and alone.
A ghost in the VCR. I rewinded it. Rewind did it.
To see little Isaac singing nursery rhymes.
The voiceover tells us.
Tells us what he's learnt, what he'll learn soon. But he looks up.
The pictures stop.

I know we would have loved him. Perhaps he would. He would.
Have loved too.
The Earth isn't ours, Brother.
Together, we sigh. We feel the weight of it all and all.
It will cease. Soon.
She will bring down the little birds.
And I will bring down the little birds.
A gorgeous oboe takes us back on a shard of light as if we are—

February

London. On a Sunday train, men and women.
Wellies are on the seats.
The world thaws. Straddling the tracks.
Fingers weave fingers.
More fingers weave fingers, on a beach in Marin County.
Gael and Diego. They've come to remember sweet Maribel.
They light a fire and sleep happy there.
Tenoch rises. Embraces them.

Some days pass. A reading at the Swedenborg.
I am alone amongst poets.
Like an egg on the end of a thread.
Eyes drop.
Tinnitus.
You agree to meet me, Brother.

Soho House is teeming and fecund.
Dervishes play billiards in perfect circles.
We devour the Brie. You know I hate Brie.
Emma Watson sits by us. Her friend wants it so bad.
Or not.
You break first.

You say, "I'm an actor too, of fire and water".
As you drink white wine.
"Waking nature. That's the rose of it.
Like lichen beneath the Arctic ice, it remains. Or remains."
She looks impressed, or tired of pizza.
I suck on an empty straw.
Only the faithful hold this place green, Brother.
Only the faithful hold this place green.

As you drive me home, you pause.
You tell me that you admired me, even envied me.
Something about lifelines.
The remnants.
The soft glow of the Northern Lights in an age of Mongers.
Or some other pish.
The moon bathes nude in the black.
I long for Judah.

The whirr of the road gives us and around us gives way.
After a while, we hear strings.
A cavernous hymn.
An echo of sounds sprawling, Brother.
Estranged.
Or it could have been a—

September

Jerusalem. All streets end here. There is this western wall.
Confronted by a dome and a rock.
Dripped in sweat.
Biblical mopeds skid in the dust. It feels hopeless, Brother.
I don't know anything anymore. I'm a guest here, amongst Glyths.
Lilith isn't enough.
I gabble my beliefs. Jesus scares, except in the corner.
His tears and lashes are on a stone.

I climb to the top of the world. Kipat Hasela.
I know. I know I stut her, Brother.
I fail.
A continuous conviction that Poesy is some sort of goddess.
It's all well-tended garbage.
Like the sea shouting.

At least here, I'm still here.
Like Abraham and his children.
We're all in it.
In pieces.
My head cracks.
Bleeding against the bricks at the bottom of the hill.

But that frail lyric.
Man, it still amazes me.
Mongst the buzz of Muezzins.
Even the walls vibrate.
Human beings are electric too, Brother.
Later. I find her in the courtyard, sipping mint tea.
A little bit at a time.
Things are.

That night, I remember Death.
A million miles away. And yes, it seems far-fetched.
Like an Arab love-myth stitched through a well-worn gillim.
Like a warm San Francisco. Tempting but illusive.
You were right, Brother.
But it's still there. Around me.

From Death comes Life.
As a series of pageants in lace.
As kestrels on the edge, fighting with their heads to the sky.
As a dark-haired girl curving on a circus swing.
As the smoke of the bonny young men, clinging to a public wall.
As a single thought. Multiplied.
It feigns as much as it alludes. It makes us lull.
Even in the cloudscape. It makes us—

October

London. Driving through it at night.
Mount Sinai is watching us.
The north against the south.
Dancing with a long straight steel frame to a punctum.
Together, things are.
The Gherkin is closing. The Eagle is closing. Streetlamps
       flickering, waining.
A timed distract.
Praising enemies in strange churches.

We had seen you that night, Brother.
You roared.
Cymbeline in chains and on a polished black stage.
An animal face.
A series of murmurs and tensed half-breaths.
Majestic. Simple.

After the show, we toast you.
But you brood.
You say, "I may be really foolish, Mike. But the sounds were
    man-made.
They seemed linked.
From another place and time.
With their own props."

The roads are hot again. Cluttered. Recurrent concrete.
Th umps.
Our windows are low.
It all seems to matter for one night only.
The air is all-but pregnant now.
Let dawn find us.
Let the prince takes us there.
We sing for Samuel sleeping in his cot, dreaming of Israel.

It seems close.
As though the towers have surrounded us.
A hot copper thread.
As we cross the bridge, we think of you, Brother.

LIGHTS, ELECTRICITY, SOUNDS AND VOICES ARE JUST WAVES.
MOTIONS. UNDUE ELATIONS AND VIBRANTS.
ANIMATE AND INTIMATE. SPIRITUAL AND MINISCULE.
PRAYERS, IF YOU WILL.

It hurts us, all of us, as we rattle across the bridge.
But the voice of Eli is in this place.
I too.
His depth, his thought-tinted musicality.
It makes me smile again. Recall.
The amber and the—

Epistle of St Paul to the Philippians

sit with me . here on the ledge
in abundance
as the winter groundswell rolls . under us and then under us

you . with red raw palms
both of us . gripping the flag tight
and the lord dancing and digging in . for any bird that swoops
and dies

will leave this place . to the spectral rats
or the giant donkeys of the shitty centre
but purples remain . as do the lanterns . paper and fire

and we remain
brothers sisters in sanctuary . in a shout of virtue or praise or
good will . we persist

as revenants

Salaam Aleikum

peace be with you

that means . something
not say hello . because you do
or nor . some secret grasp
the ant scrapens in the dust . doost

but see the gift
it smithed by and by . heateded
cradle carried . these blisters
to lovingly exchange . in the dark

to give to you . and me
a greet in . so
we . need never . h
for fea . fears . es

of its absence

A Stone with a Hole in It

on a childish beach
it keeps us us . away . evil shaytaans
(wonder if they get it)
a stone . with a hole in it
keeps us us . away . with shaytaans
(is what it is . sorry)

quie . t . idyll . s
but a void . restless
(sigh and move a head)
of bad bad progress . on shore

then he realises
surround is done . like a whole way of life
neared to the edge
(mistake i . never mentioned)
it . neared to the edge

so begin in . shoroo
feel and keep us . local things are alike
(la aa eik)
a stone . with a hole in it

East Jerusalem Blues

brother . these are our blues
up and in the walls . sheets
stick . wafting in the wind
there are no territories here
for the rats . for the blues
along the dark thin streets
solomon burke sits . drinks tea
the scent of jesus . the screams
of lots of girls and lots of boys
yes the market teems brother
ashara ashara . love of ashara
swamps an open concourse

yet we are closed . they inside
habibi . a frail lyric . is blues
like a gentle bang on the head
or rotting sharon fruits . or you
left and broken by the barrow boys
no coins just kisses . they laugh
playing football by the gates
to the sound of the west bank bus
making it the blues . for the ashara
blues . for the love of ashara

The Old Gaza Road

is gone to . you
blocked in . once
but i just . there
promise of . you
enough for a . now
soldiers do . now
prism and . once
connate the . torn
if only i . the sea
bit by bit . sounds
taste a . and again
slowly i . memory
i cou . back then
a light breeze . a
habibi means . you
strawberries . but
like a . a . in the

then i would love to
even if it were
when it was men
a quantity of truth
stretched with a
cross on his back

Sobh Bekheyr Azizam
("The Good Morrow")

lost in the dark immensity of her eyes
he was drawn in . like a honey bee
i guess he must have loved her
to have flown there . leaving his world
sphere against sphere . in a dream
of one little room . beside another
and he circled . turning to this moon
fixed on those breathless eyes
basking like a thief with nightgold

oh john . I'm so sorry . you were wrong
our friend haafez should have told you this
you see your face reflects . not refracts
it's like a thin film . an unequal mix

divided . seeded with the threats and lullabies of wine and whisky

Nesf e Jahaan
("half the world")

he said . we men we
half / the world
as he boiled tea
on a tiny gas stove

we slip our tongues
in (to) their mouths
set / sweet / knees
but isfahan evinces us

like a plastic jar of coins

There Was Once a Leaf

with veins . strands
with each other . de coeur

it danced . turned
was . as ore . lit up
in and out . of the sun

it blotted the earth
as it skipped
catching a drop or two

skirting . in . this place
spits . and slits

honest . worthy . de coeur
from an unknown tree

and at the end . when it fell
there were new roots
from the stretch . the sky
breaking the earth

Help Wither This Fight

man i am tired of advocates
of the them actually
i don't hate them . no
quite the opposite
it's quite beyond them
like a sphere or a suffix
of praxis . of schism
to explain the absence
of soldiers . law courts
waged on women or
attendants of life or
widows of money . guns and guns

man i am tired of the sweep
run them in circles . scatter
but never let them go
never let them deepen
grip hold of each fibre
like forough or emmeline
like the ghost of noor
like the priests of the sun
the sea flags are aligned
blowing in the gusts
blowing for the gusts

for us as an i or a we
we urge you
you . as a man or men
to be difficult . complex
a grievance propellor
not colour me by numbers or
make me glitter . in spirit
deaf . deaf . deaf . de
to a choice of each evil

for us as an i or a we
living breathing breasts or
brutal question marks
with a baby that cries or
an end . end less politics
papers soaked in snow
from the beginning it is
as she smiles for us both
of a cat and a mouse
for the future . is going . is
to help wither this fight

www.ingramcontent.com/pod-product-compliance
Lightning Source LLC
Chambersburg PA
CBHW021949040426
42448CB00008B/1321